Hippocrene
CHILDREN'S
ILLUSTRATED
POLISH
DICTIONARY

ENGLISH - POLISH
POLISH - ENGLISH

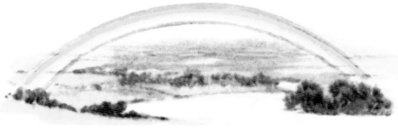

D1089577

Compiled and translated by the Editors of Hippocrene Books

Interior illustrations by S. Grant (24, 81, 88); J. Gress (page 10, 21, 24, 37, 46, 54, 59, 65, 72, 75, 77);
K. Migliorelli (page 13, 14, 18, 19, 20, 21, 22, 25, 31, 32, 37, 39, 40, 46, 47, 66, 71, 75, 76, 82, 86, 87);
B. Swidzinska (page 9, 11, 12, 13, 14, 16, 23, 27, 28, 30, 32, 33, 35, 37, 38, 41, 42, 45, 46, 47, 48, 49, 50,
52, 53, 56, 57, 58, 59, 60, 61, 62, 63, 66, 68, 69, 70, 71, 72, 73, 75, 77, 78, 79, 83), N. Zhukov (page 8, 13,
14, 17, 18, 23, 27, 29, 33, 34, 39, 40, 41, 52, 64, 65, 71, 72, 73, 78, 84, 86, 88).

Design, prepress, and production: Graafiset International, Inc.

Cataloging-in-Publication Data available from the Library of Congress.

ISBN 0-7818-0711-5 (Hardcover edition, 1999)
ISBN 0-7818-0890-1 (Paperback edition, 2002)

Printed in Hong Kong.

For information, address:
Hippocrene Books, Inc.
171 Madison Avenue
New York, NY 10016

INTRODUCTION

With their absorbent minds, infinite curiosities and excellent memories, children have enormous capacities to master many languages. All they need is exposure and encouragement.

The easiest way to learn a foreign language is to simulate the same natural method by which a child learns English. The natural technique is built on the concept that language is representational of concrete objects and ideas. The use of pictures and words are the natural way for children to begin to acquire a new language.

The concept of this Illustrated Dictionary is to allow children to build vocabulary and initial competency naturally. Looking at the pictorial content of the Dictionary and saying and matching the words in connection to the drawings gives children the opportunity to discover the foreign language and thus, a new way to communicate.

The drawings in the Dictionary are designed to capture children's imaginations and make the learning process interesting and entertaining, as children return to a word and picture repeatedly until they begin to recognize it.

The beautiful images and clear presentation make this dictionary a wonderful tool for unlocking your child's multilingual potential.

**Deborah Dumont, M.A., M.Ed.,
Child Psychologist and Educational Consultant**

Polish Pronunciation

In Polish, vowels and consonants are clearly pronounced, and their pronunciation and division into syllables varies. The phonetic transcriptions used in this dictionary suggest the pronunciation that is close to the original and at the same time easiest to enunciate for an English reader. The transcriptions are divided into syllables. The accent usually falls on the next to the last syllable.

Vowels

a = as **a** in *half*
o = as **o** in *November*
u, ó = as **oo** in *food*
e = as **e** in *get*
i = as **ee** in *meet*
y = as **i** in *bit*
ą , ę = varies depending upon position in a word. In the middle of a word the vowel "ą" is transcribed as **on** or **om**; the vowel "ę" is marked as **en** or **em**. At the end of a word, the "ą" sounds close to the nasal French "**on**" in *bon appétit*; while the vowel "ę" in the same position could be pronounced as a clear "**e**" as in *self*.

Consonants

Many Polish consonants are pronounced as in English. The following are pronounced differently:

c = as English **ts** in *cats*
cz = as **ch** in *church* but harder
ć, ci = as **t** in *nature* but softer
ch, h = as **h** in *ham*
dz = as **ds** in *ads*
dź, dzi = as **j** in *jeep*
dż = as **dg** in *dodge* but harder
j = as **y** in *yes*
ł = as **w** in *was*
sz = as **sh** in *shake* but harder
ś si = as **s** in *sure* but softer
w = as **v** in *very*
ź, zi = as **z** in *zero* but softer
ż, rz = as **s** in *measure*

airplane   **samolot**
sa-mo-lot

alligator   **aligator**
a-li-ga-tor

alphabet   **alfabet**
al-fa-bet

antelope   **antylopa**
an-ti-loh-pa

antlers   **rogi jelenie**
roh-gee ye-le-nye

apple   **jabłko**
                   yap-koh

aquarium   **akwarium**
                      ak-far-yoom

arch   **sklepienie łukowe**
                  skle-pye-nieh woo-koh-veh

arrow   **strzała**
                   s-cha-wa

autumn   **jesień**
                    ye-shen

baby **dziecko**
jets-ko

backpack **plecak**
ple-tsak

badger **borsuk**
bore-sook

baker **piekarz**
pye-kash

ball **piłka**
peew-ka

balloon **balon**
ba-lon

banana   **banan**
ba-nan

barley   **jęczmień**
yench-myen

barrel   **beczka**
bech-ka

basket   **koszyk**
koh-shik

bat   **nietoperz**
nyeh-toh-pesh

beach   **plaża**
pla-zha

bear **niedźwiedź**
nedzh-vyech

beaver **bóbr**
boobr

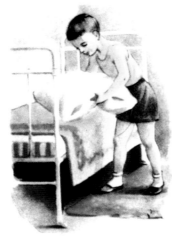

bed **łóżko**
woosh-ko

bee **pszczoła**
pshcho-wa

beetle **chrząszcz**
hshonshch

bell **dzwon**
dzvon

belt   **pas**
pas

bench   **ława**
wa-va

bicycle   **rower**
roh-ver

binoculars   **lornetka**
lor-net-ka

bird   **ptak**
ptahk

birdcage   **klatka**
klaht-ka

black　　　　**czarny**
char-ni

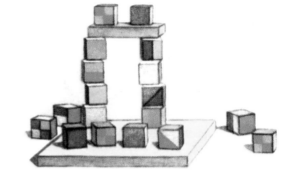

blocks　　　　**klocki**
klots-kee

blossom　　　　**kwitnąć**
kfeet-nonch

blue　　　　**niebieski**
nye-byes-kee

boat　　　　**łódka**
woot-ka

bone　　　　**kość**
koshch

book **książka**
ksonsh-ka

boot **but**
booht

bottle **butelka**
boo-tel-ka

bowl **miska**
mees-ka

boy **chłopak**
hwo-pak

bracelet **bransoletka**
bran-so-let-ka

branch   **gałąź**
                    ga-wonzh

bread   **chleb**
                   hleb

breakfast   **śniadanie**
                       shnia-da-nie

bridge   **most**
                    most

broom   **miotła**
                   myot-wa

brother   **brat**
                     braht

brown   **brązowy**
bron-zo-vi

brush   **szczotka**
shchot-ka

bucket   **wiadro**
vyad-ro

bulletin board   **tablica ogłoszeń**
tab-lee-tsa og-wo-shen

bumblebee   **trzmiel**
chmyel

butterfly   **motyl**
mo-til

cab   **taksówka**
tak-soof-ka

cabbage   **kapusta**
ka-poos-ta

cactus   **kaktus**
kak-toos

café   **kawiarnia**
kah-vyar-nya

cake   **tort**
tort

camel   **wielbłąd**
vyel-bwond

camera   **aparat fotograficzny**
a-pa-rat fo-to-gra-feech-ni

candle   **świeca**
shfye-tsa

candy   **cukierek**
tsoo-kie-rek

canoe   **kajak**
kah-yak

cap   **czapka**
chap-ka

captain   **kapitan**
ka-pee-tan

car   **samochód**
sa-mo-hood

card   **karta**
kar-ta

carpet   **dywan**
di-vahn

carrot   **marchew**
mar-hef

(to) carry   **nosić**
no-sheech

castle   **zamek**
za-mek

cat **kot**
koht

cave **grota**
groh-ta

chair **krzesło**
kshes-wo

cheese **ser**
ser

cherry **wiśnia**
veesh-nya

chimney **komin**
koh-meen

chocolate **czekolada**
che-ko-la-da

Christmas tree **choinka**
ho-een-ka

circus **cyrk**
tsirk

(to) climb **wspinać się**
fspee-nach sye

cloud **chmura**
hmoo-ra

clown **błazen**
bwa-zen

coach   **wagon**
va-gon

coat   **płaszcz**
pwashch

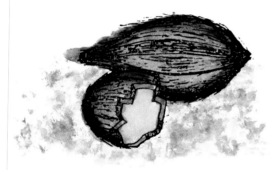

coconut   **orzech kokosowy**
o-zekh ko-ko-so-vi

comb   **grzebień**
gzhe-byen

comforter   **kołdra**
kow-dra

compass   **kompas**
kom-pas

(to) cook   **gotować**
                            go-to-vach

cork   **korek**
                            ko-rek

corn   **kukurydza**
                            koo-koo-ri-dsa

cow   **krowa**
                            kroh-va

cracker   **krakers**
                            kra-kers

cradle   **kołyska**
                            ko-wis-kah

(to) crawl   **pełzać**
pew-zach

(to) cross   **przechodzić**
psheh-ho-dyts

crown   **korona**
koh-ro-na

(to) cry   **płakać**
pwa-kach

cucumber   **ogórek**
o-goo-rek

curtain   **kurtyna**
koor-ti-na

(to) dance   **tańczyć**
                        tan-chich

dandelion   **mlecz**
                       mlech

date   **data**
                  da-ta

deer   **sarna**
                  sahr-nah

desert   **pustynia**
                    poos-ti-nya

desk   **biurko**
                  byoor-ko

dirty   **brudny**
                   brood-ni

dog

pies
pyes

doghouse

psia buda
psya boo-da

doll

lalka
lal-ka

dollhouse

dom lalek
dom la-lek

dolphin

delfin
del-feen

donkey

osioł
o-show

dragon

smok
smok

dragonfly   **ważka**
                       vash-ka

(to) draw   **rysować**
                       ri-soh-vach

dress   **sukienka**
                       soo-kyen-ka

(to) drink   **pić**
                       peech

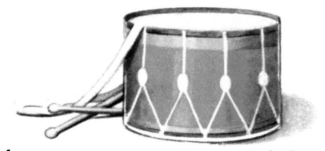

drum   **bęben**
                       ben-ben

duck   **kaczka**
                       kach-ka

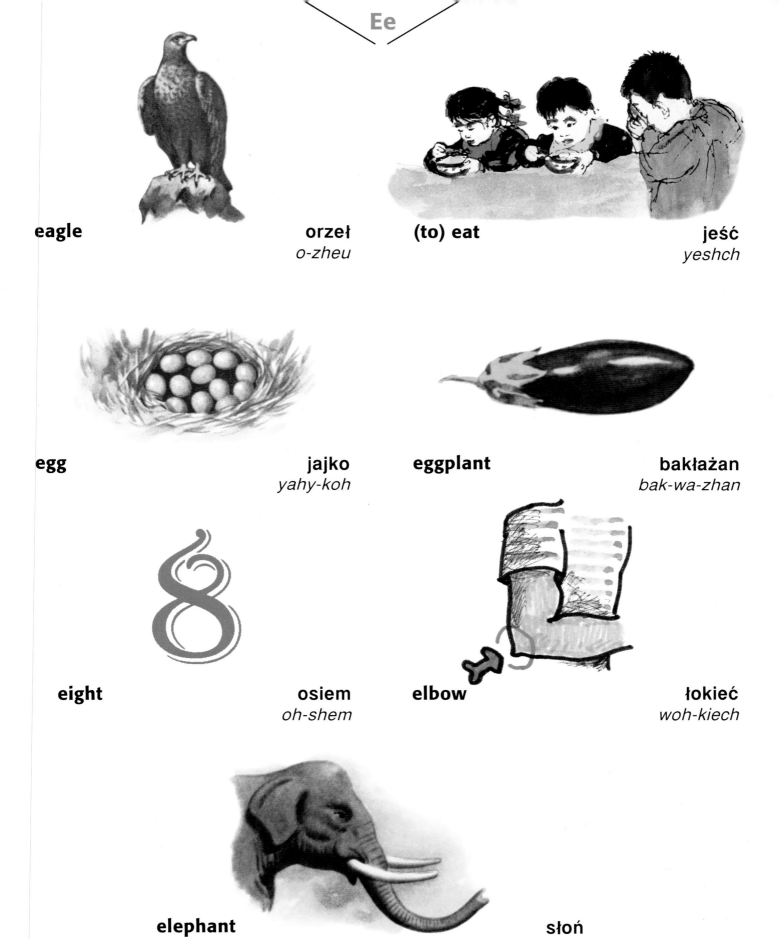

Ee

eagle — **orzeł** *o-zheu*

(to) eat — **jeść** *yeshch*

egg — **jajko** *yahy-koh*

eggplant — **bakłażan** *bak-wa-zhan*

eight — **osiem** *oh-shem*

elbow — **łokieć** *woh-kiech*

elephant — **słoń** *swon*

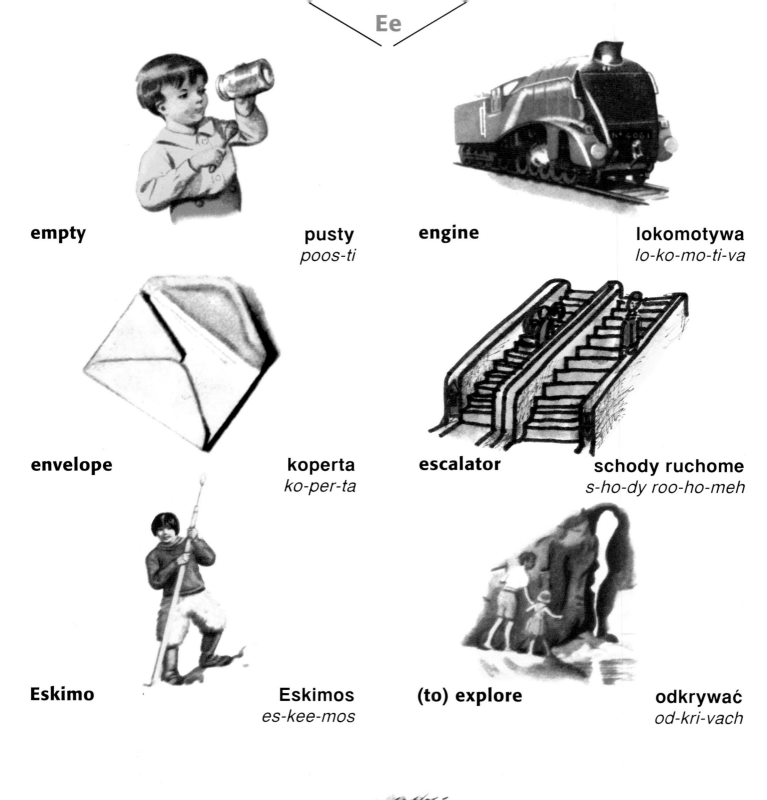

empty   **pusty**
poos-ti

engine   **lokomotywa**
lo-ko-mo-ti-va

envelope   **koperta**
ko-per-ta

escalator   **schody ruchome**
s-ho-dy roo-ho-meh

Eskimo   **Eskimos**
es-kee-mos

(to) explore   **odkrywać**
od-kri-vach

eye   **oko**
oh-koh

face　　　　　**twarz**
　　　　　　　　　tfash

fan　　　　　**wiatrak**
　　　　　　　vyat-rak

father　　　　　**ojciec**
　　　　　　　　oy-chets

fear　　　　　**strach**
　　　　　　　strakh

feather　　　　　**pióro**
　　　　　　　　pyoo-ro

(to) feed　　　　　**karmić**
　　　　　　　　kar-meech

fence   **płot**
pwot

fern   **paproć**
pa-proch

field   **pole**
poh-leh

field mouse   **mysz polna**
mish pol-na

finger   **palec**
pah-lets

fir tree   **jodła**
yod-wa

fire ogień
o-gien

fish **ryba**
ri-ba

(to) fish łowić
woh-veech

fist pięść
pyenshch

five pięć
pyench

flag **flaga**
fla-ga

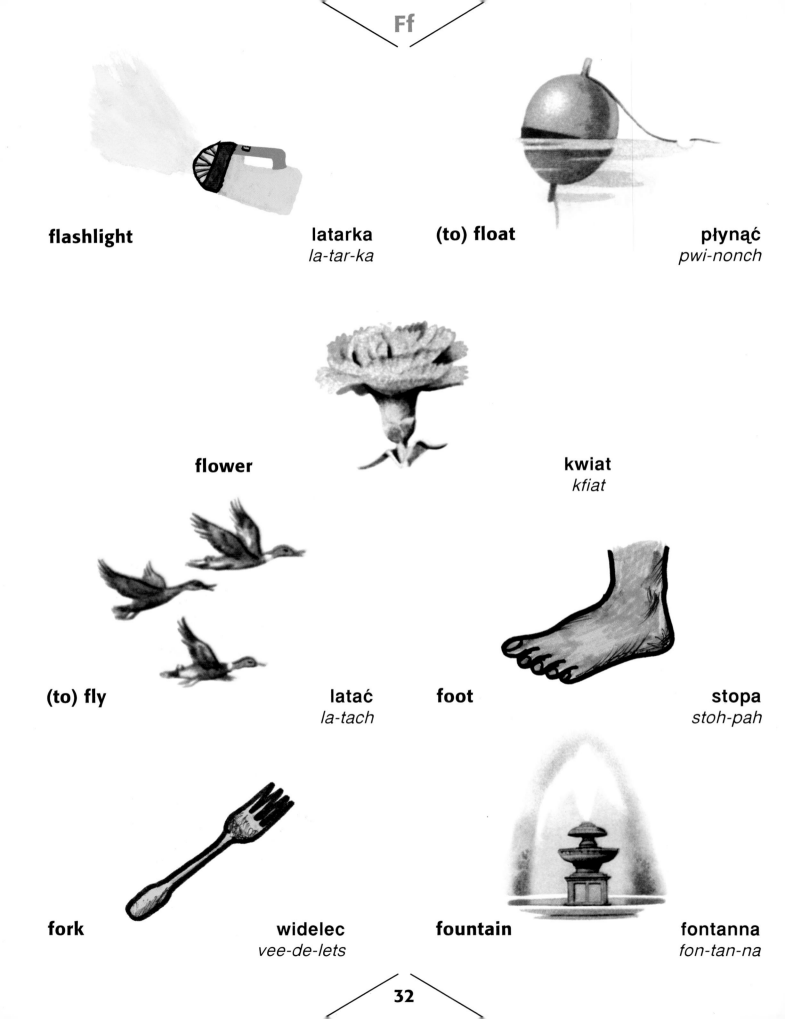

flashlight   **latarka**
la-tar-ka

(to) float   **płynąć**
pwi-nonch

flower   **kwiat**
kfiat

(to) fly   **latać**
la-tach

foot   **stopa**
stoh-pah

fork   **widelec**
vee-de-lets

fountain   **fontanna**
fon-tan-na

four   **cztery**
chte-ri

fox   **lis**
lees

frame   **ramka**
ram-ka

friend   **kolega**
koh-leh-gah

frog   **żaba**
zha-ba

fruit   **owoce**
oh-voh-tse

furniture   **meble**
meb-leh

garden **ogród**
oh-groot

gate **brama**
bra-ma

(to) gather **zbierać**
zbye-rach

geranium **geranium**
ge-ra-ni-um

giraffe **żyrafa**
zhi-ra-fa

girl **dziewczyna**
dzhef-chi-na

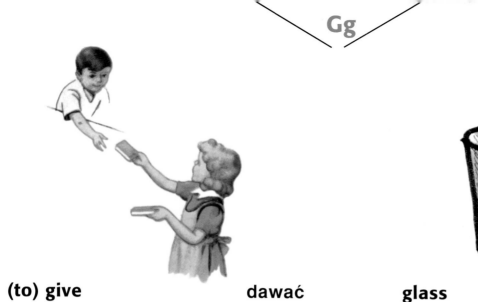

(to) give   **dawać**
da-vach

glass   **szklanka**
shklan-ka

glasses   **okulary**
oh-koo-lah-ri

globe   **glob**
glop

glove   **rękawiczka**
ren-ka-veech-ka

goat   **kozioł**
kozh-ow

goldfish **złota rybka**
zwo-tah rip-kah

"Good Night" **"dobranoc"**
do-bra-nots

"Good-bye" **"do widzenia"**
do vee-dze-nya

goose **gęś**
gensh

grandfather **dziadek**
dzha-dek

grandmother **babcia**
bab-cha

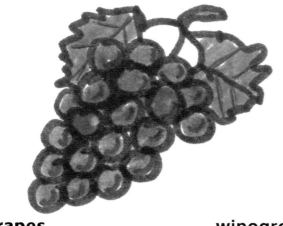

grapes　　　　**winogrona**
vee-no-gro-na

grasshopper　　　　**konik polny**
ko-neek pol-ni

green　　　　**zielony**
zhe-lo-ni

greenhouse　　　　**cieplarnia**
chep-lar-nia

guitar　　　　**gitara**
gee-ta-ra

hammer   **młotek**
mwo-tek

hammock   **hamak**
hah-mak

hamster   **chomik**
hoh-meek

hand   **ręka**
ren-ka

handbag   **torebka damska**
toh-rep-ka dam-ska

handkerchief   **chusteczka do nosa**
hoos-tech-ka doh noh-sa

harvest **żniwa**
zhnee-va

hat **kapelusz**
ka-peh-loosh

hay **siano**
sha-no

headdress **pióropusz**
pyoo-ro-poosh

heart **serce**
ser-tse

hedgehog **jeż**
yesh

hen **kura**
koo-ra

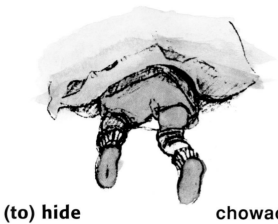

(to) hide **chować się**
ho-vach sye

highway **autostrada**
au-to-stra-da

honey **miód**
myoot

horns **rogi**
roh-gee

horse **koń**
koyn

horseshoe

podkowa
pot-koh-vah

hourglass

klepsydra
klep-si-dra

house

dom
dom

(to) hug

uścisnąć
oo-shees-nonch

hydrant

hydrant
hid-rant

Ii

ice cream **lody**
loh-di

ice cubes **kostki lodu**
kost-kee loh-doo

ice-skating **jeździć na łyżwach**
yez-dzeets nah wizh-vakh

instrument **instrument**
een-stroo-ment

iris **irys**
ee-ris

iron **żelazko**
zhe-las-zo

island **wyspa**
vis-pa

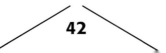

jacket **żakiet**
zha-kyet

jam **dżem**
jem

jigsaw puzzle **składanka**
skwa-dan-ka

jockey **dżokej**
jok-kehy

juggler **kuglarz**
koog-lash

(to) jump **skoczyć**
skoh-chich

kangaroo   **kangur**
kan-goor

key   **klucz**
klooch

kitten   **kotek**
koh-tek

knife   **nóż**
noosh

knight   **rycerz**
ri-tsesh

(to) knit   **robić na drutach**
ro-beech nah droo-tah

knot   **węzeł**
ven-zehw

koala bear   **koala**
ko-a-la

ladder   **drabina**
dra-bee-na

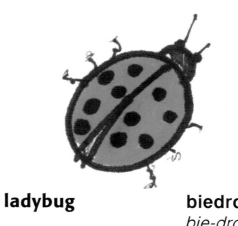

ladybug   **biedronka**
bie-dron-ka

lamb   **baranek**
ba-ra-nek

lamp   **lampa**
lam-pa

(to) lap   **chłeptać**
hwep-tach

laughter   **śmiech**
shmyeh

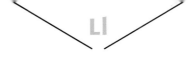
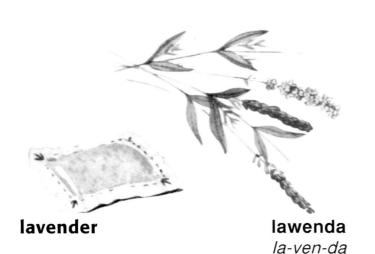

lavender   **lawenda**
                      la-ven-da

lawn mower   **kosiarka**
                      koh-shar-ka

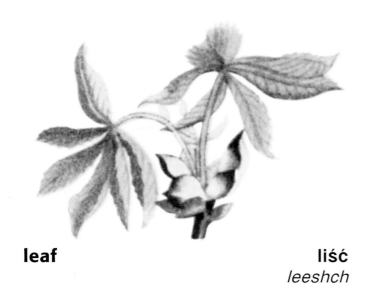

leaf   **liść**
                      leeshch

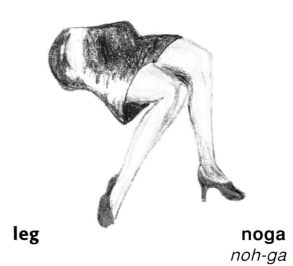

leg   **noga**
                      noh-ga

lemon   **cytryna**
                      tsi-tri-na

lettuce   **sałata**
                      sa-wa-ta

lightbulb   **żarówka**
zha-roof-ka

lighthouse   **latarnia morska**
la-tar-nia mor-ska

lilac   **bez**
bes

lion   **lew**
lef

(to) listen   **słuchać**
swoo-hach

lobster   **homar**
hoh-mar

Ll

lock   **zamek**
za-mek

lovebird   **papużka**
pa-poosh-ka

luggage   **bagaż**
ba-gash

lumberjack   **drwal**
drval

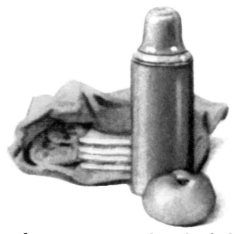

lunch   **drugie śniadanie**
droo-gye shnya-da-nye

lynx   **ryś**
rish

magazine   **magazyn**
ma-ga-zin

magician   **magik**
ma-geek

magnet   **magnes**
mag-nes

map   **mapa**
ma-pa

maple leaf   **liść klonu**
leesch kloh-nu

marketplace   **rynek**
ri-nek

mask   **maska**
mas-ka

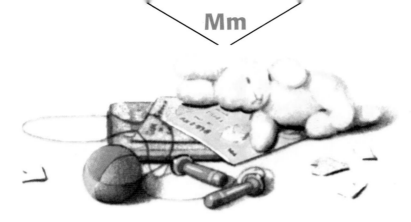

messy

niechlujny
nyeh-looy-ni

milkman

mleczarz
mle-chash

mirror

lustro
loos-troh

mitten

rękawiczka
ren-ka-veech-ka

money

pieniądze
pye-non-tse

monkey

małpa
maw-pa

moon

księżyc
kshen-zhits

mother

matka
mat-ka

mountain

góra
goo-ra

mouse

mysz
mish

mouth

usta
oos-ta

mushroom

grzyb
gzhip

music

muzyka
moo-zi-ka

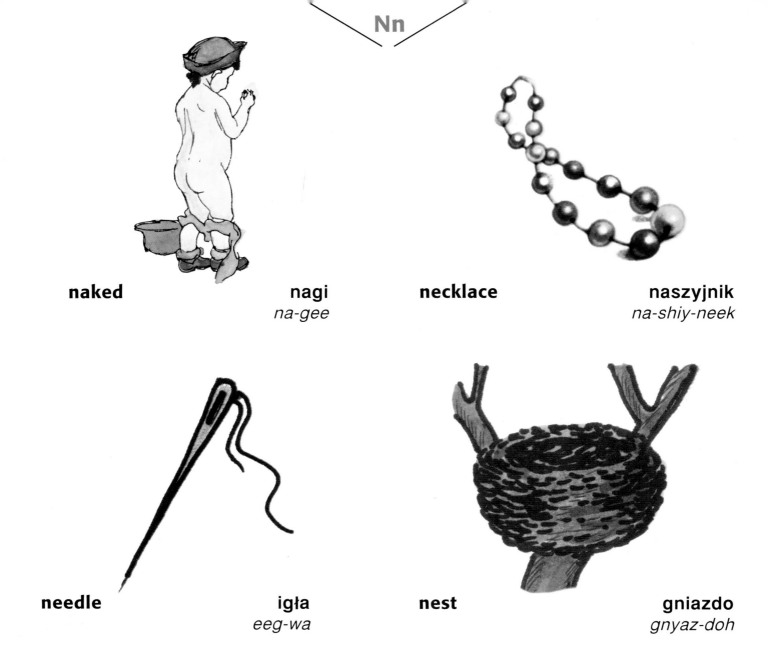

naked   **nagi**
na-gee

necklace   **naszyjnik**
na-shiy-neek

needle   **igła**
eeg-wa

nest   **gniazdo**
gnyaz-doh

newspaper   **gazeta**
ga-ze-ta

nightingale

słowik
swo-veek

nine

dziewięć
dzhe-vyench

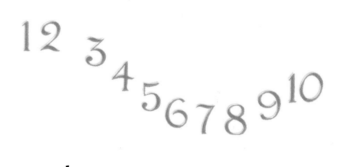

notebook

zeszyt
ze-shit

number

numer
noo-mer

nut

orzech
oh-zheh

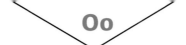

oar   **wiosło**
vyos-wo

ocean liner   **statek oceaniczny**
sta-tek oh-tse-ah-neech-ni

old   **stary**
stah-ri

one   **jeden**
ye-den

onion   **cebula**
tse-boo-la

open   **otwarty**
oh-tfar-ti

orange   **pomarańcza**
po-ma-ran-cha

ostrich   **struś**
stroosh

owl   **sowa**
soh-va

ox   **wół**
voow

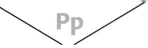

padlock　　　**kłódka**
kwoot-ka

paint　　　**farba**
far-ba

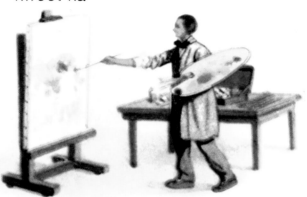

painter　　　**malarz**
ma-lash

pajamas　　　**piżama**
pee-zha-ma

palm tree　　　**palma**
pal-ma

paper　　　**papier**
pa-pyer

parachute　　　**spadochron**
spa-do-hron

park

park
park

parrot   **papuga**
pa-poo-ga

passport   **paszport**
pash-port

patch   **łata**
wa-ta

path   **ścieżka**
schyesh-ka

peach   **brzoskwinia**
bzhos-kfee-nya

pear   **gruszka**
groo-shka

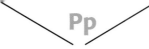

pebble **kamyk**
kam-ik

(to) peck **dziobać**
dzho-bach

(to) peel **obrać**
ob-rach

ołówek
oh-woo-vek

pelican **pelikan**
pe-lee-kan

pencil

penguin **pingwin**
peen-gveen

people **ludzie**
loo-dzye

piano | **pianino**
pya-nee-no

pickle | **ogórek kiszony**
o-goo-rek kee-sho-ni

pie | **placek**
pla-tsek

pig | **świnia**
shfee-nya

pigeon | **gołąb**
go-womp

pillow | **poduszka**
po-doosh-ka

pin | **szpilka**
shpeel-ka

pine   **sosna**
sos-na

pineapple   **ananas**
a-na-nas

pit   **pestka**
pest-ka

pitcher   **dzbanek**
dzba-nek

plate   **talerz**
ta-lesh

platypus   **dziobak**
dzho-bak

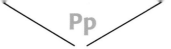

(to) play grać
grach

plum śliwka
shleef-ka

polar bear biały niedźwiedź
bya-wy nedzh-vyech

pony kucyk
koo-tsik

pot garnek
gar-nek

potato ziemniak
zhem-niak

(to) pour　　　　**wlewać**
vleh-vach

present　　　　**prezent**
pre-zent

(to) pull　　　　**ciągnąć**
chong-nonch

pumpkin　　　　**dynia**
di-nya

puppy　　　　**szczeniak**
shche-niak

queen　　　　**królowa**
kroo-loh-vah

rabbit

królik
kroo-leek

raccoon

szop
shop

racket

rakieta
ra-kie-ta

radio

radio
ra-dyo

radish

rzodkiewka
zhod-kyef-ka

raft **tratwa**
trat-fa

rain **deszcz**
deshch

rainbow **tęcza**
ten-cha

raincoat **płaszcz nieprzemakalny**
pwashch nie-pzhe-ma-kal-ni

raspberry **malina**
ma-lee-na

(to) read   **czytać**
chi-tach

red   **czerwony**
cher-voh-ni

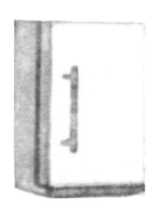

refrigerator   **lodówka**
lo-doof-ka

rhinoceros   **nosorożec**
noh-soh-roh-zhets

ring   **pierścień**
pyersh-chen

(to) ring dzwonić
dzvo-neech

river rzeka
zhe-ka

road droga
dro-ga

rocket rakieta
ra-kie-ta

roof dach
dakh

rooster kogut
koh-goot

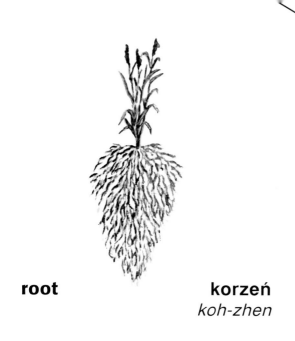

root　　　　**korzeń**
koh-zhen

rope　　　　**sznur**
schnoor

rose　　　　**róża**
roo-zha

(to) row　　　　**wiosłować**
vyos-woh-vach

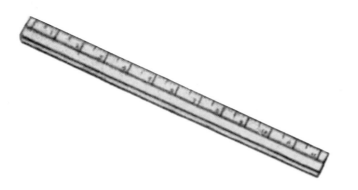

ruler　　　　**linijka**
lee-neey-ka

(to) run　　　　**biegać**
byeh-gach

safety pin   **agrafka**
a-graf-ka

(to) sail   **żeglować**
zhe-glo-vach

sailor   **marynarz**
ma-ri-nash

salt   **sól**
sool

scarf   **szalik**
sha-leek

school   **szkoła**
shko-wa

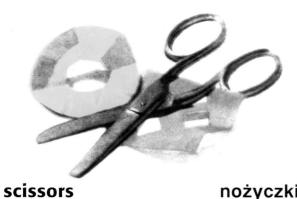

scissors **nożyczki**
noh-zhi-chkee

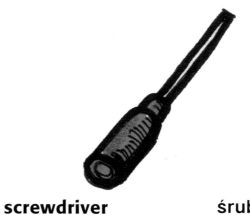

screwdriver **śrubokręt**
shroo-bo-krent

seagull **mewa**
me-va

seesaw **huśtawka**
hoosh-taf-ka

seven **siedem**
shie-dem

(to) sew **szyć**
shich

shark　　　**rekin**
reh-keen

sheep　　　**owca**
of-tsa

shell　　　**muszla**
moosh-la

shepherd　　　**pasterz**
pas-tesh

ship　　　**statek**
sta-tek

shirt　　　**koszula**
ko-shoo-la

shoe

but
boot

shovel

łopata
wo-pa-ta

(to) show

pokazywać
po-ka-zi-vach

shower

prysznic
prish-neets

shutter

okiennice
oh-kyen-nee-tse

sick

chory
hoh-ri

sieve   **sito**
shee-toh

(to) sing   **śpiewać**
shpyeh-vach

(to) sit   **siadać**
sha-dach

six   **sześć**
sheshch

sled   **sanki**
san-kee

(to) sleep   **spać**
spach

small   **mały**
mah-wi

smile   **uśmiech**
oosh-mieh

snail   **ślimak**
shlee-mak

snake   **wąż**
vonsh

snow   **śnieg**
shnyek

sock   **skarpeta**
skar-pe-ta

sofa   **kanapa**
ka-na-pa

sparrow   **wróbel**
vroo-bel

spider   **pająk**
pa-yonk

spiderweb   **pajęczyna**
pa-yen-chi-na

spoon   **łyżka**
wizh-ka

squirrel   **wiewiórka**
vye-vyoor-ka

stairs   **schody**
s-ho-di

stamp   **znaczek**
zna-chek

starfish   **rozgwiazda**
roz-gvyaz-da

stork   **bocian**
bo-chan

stove   **piec**
pyets

strawberry   **truskawka**
troos-kaf-ka

subway

metro
me-tro

sugar cube   **cukier w kostkach**
tsoo-kier v kost-kah

sun

słońce
swon-tse

sunflower   **słonecznik**
swo-nech-neek

sweater

sweter
sfe-ter

(to) sweep   **zamiatać**
za-mya-tach

swing

huśtawka
hoosh-taf-ka

table **stół**
stoow

teapot **czajnik**
chay-neek

teddy bear **miś**
meesh

television **telewizja**
te-le-veez-ya

10

ten **dziesięć**
jeh-shyents

tent **namiot**
na-myot

theater   **teatr**
te-atr

thimble   **naparstek**
na-par-stek

(to) think   **myśleć**
mish-lech

three   **trzy**
tzhi

tie   **krawat**
kra-vat

(to) tie   **wiązać**
vyown-zach

tiger   **tygrys**
tig-ris

toaster   **toster**
toh-ster

tomato   **pomidor**
po-mee-dor

toucan   **tukan**
too-kan

towel   **ręcznik**
rench-neek

tower   **wieża**
vye-zha

toy box   **pudełko na zabawki**
poo-dew-ko nah zah-baf-kee

tracks   **szyny**
shih-nih

train station   **dworzec**
dvoh-zhets

tray   **taca**
ta-tsa

tree   **drzewo**
dzhe-voh

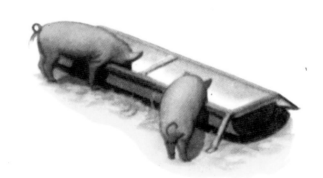

trough   **koryto**
ko-ri-toh

truck

ciężarówka
chen-zhar-roof-kah

trumpet   **trąbka**
tromp-ka

tulip   **tulipan**
too-lee-pan

tunnel   **tunel**
too-nel

turtle   **żółw**
zhoowf

twins   **bliźniaczki**
bleez-nyach-kee

two   **dwa**
dva

umbrella   **parasol**   **uphill**   **w górę**
pa-ra-sol   *v goor-eh*

Vv

vase   **waza**   **veil**   **welon**
va-za   *veh-lon*

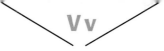

village

wieś
vyesh

violet

fiołek
fyo-wek

violin

skrzypce
skship-tse

voyage

podróż
pod-roosh

waiter — **kelner**
kel-ner

(to) wake up — **obudzić (się)**
o-boo-dzheech (sye)

walrus — **mors**
mors

(to) wash — **prać**
prach

watch — **zegarek**
ze-ga-rek

(to) watch — **oglądać**
oglon-dach

(to) water   **podlewać**
pod-leh-vach

waterfall   **wodospad**
voh-doh-spat

watering can   **konewka**
koh-nef-ka

watermelon   **arbuz**
ar-boos

weather vane   **wiatrowskaz**
vya-troh-fskas

(to) weigh   **ważyć**
va-zhich

whale   **wieloryb**
vye-lo-rib

wheel   **koło**
koh-woh

wheelbarrow   **taczka**
tach-ka

whiskers   **wąsy**
von-si

(to) whisper   **szeptać**
shep-tach

whistle   **gwizdek**
gveez-dek

white   **biały**
                 bya-wi

wig   **peruka**
                 pe-roo-ka

wind   **wiatr**
                 vyatr

window   **okno**
                 ok-no

wings   **skrzydła**
                 skshid-wa

winter   **zima**
                 zhee-ma

wolf

wilk
veelk

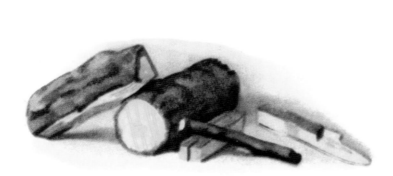

wood　　　　**drewno**
drev-no

word　　　　**słowo**
swoh-voh

(to) write

pisać
pee-sach

yellow   **żółty**
                             zhoow-ti

zebra   **zebra**
                             zeh-bra

A

agrafka safety pin
akwarium aquarium
alfabet alphabet
aligator alligator
ananas pineapple
antylopa antelope
aparat fotograficzny camera
arbuz watermelon
autostrada highway

B

babcia grandmother
bagaż luggage
bakłażan eggplant
balon balloon
banan banana
baranek lamb
beczka barrel
bez lilac
bęben drum
biały white
biały niedźwiedź polar bear
biedronka ladybug
biegać (to) run
biurko desk
bliźniaczki twins
błazen clown
bocian stork
borsuk badger
bóbr beaver
brama gate
bransoletka bracelet
brat brother
brązowy brown
brudny dirty
brzoskwinia peach
but boot; shoe
butelka bottle

C

cebula onion
chleb bread
chłeptać (to) lap
chłopak boy
chmura cloud
choinka Christmas tree
chomik hamster
chować się (to hide)
chory sick
chrząszcz beetle
chusteczka do nosa handkerchief
ciągnąć (to) pull
cieplarnia greenhouse
ciężarówka truck
cukier w kostkach sugar cube
cukierek candy
cyrk circus
cytryna lemon
czajnik teapot
czapka cap
czarny black
czekolada chocolate
czerwony red
cztery four
czytać (to) read

D

dach roof
data date
dawać (to) give
delfin dolphin
deszcz rain
dobranoc "Good night"
dom house
dom lalek dollhouse
do widzenia "Good-bye"
drabina ladder
drewno wood
droga road
drugie śniadanie lunch
drwal lumberjack
drzewo tree
dwa two
dworzec train station

dynia pumpkin
dywan carpet
dzbanek pitcher
dziadek grandfather
dziecko baby
dziesięć ten
dziewczyna girl
dziewięć nine
dziobać (to) peck
dziobak platypus
dzwon bell
dzwonić (to) ring
dżem jam
dżokej jockey

E

Eskimos Eskimo

F

farba paint
fiołek violet
flaga flag
fontanna fountain

G

garnek pot
gazeta newspaper
gałąź branch
geranium geranium
gęś goose
gitara guitar
glob globe
gniazdo nest
gotować (to) cook
gołąb pigeon
góra mountain
grać (to) play
grota cave
gruszka pear

grzebień comb
grzyb mushroom
gwizdek whistle

H

hamak hammock
homar lobster
huśtawka seesaw; swing
hydrant hydrant

I

igła needle
instrument instrument
irys iris

J

jabłko apple
jajko egg
jeden one
jesień autumn
jeść (to) eat
jeździć na łyżwach ice-skating
jeż hedgehog
jęczmień barley
jodła fir tree

K

kaczka duck
kajak canoe
kaktus cactus
kamyk pebble
kanapa sofa
kangur kangaroo
kapelusz hat
kapitan captain
kapusta cabbage
karmić (to) feed
karta card
kawiarnia café
kelner waiter

klatka birdcage
klepsydra hourglass
klocki blocks
klucz key
kłódka padlock
koala koala bear
kogut rooster
kolega friend
komin chimney
kompas compass
konewka watering can
konik polny grasshopper
koń horse
kość bone
koperta envelope
korek cork
korona crown
koryto trough
korzeń root
kosiarka lawn mower
kostki lodu ice cubes
koszula shirt
koszyk basket
kot cat
kotek kitten
kozioł goat
kołdra comforter
koło wheel
kołyska cradle
krakers cracker
krawat tie
krowa cow
królik rabbit
królowa queen
krzesło chair
księżyc moon
książka book
kucyk pony
kuglarz juggler
kukurydza corn
kura hen
kurtyna curtain
kwiat flower
kwitnąć blossom

L

lalka doll
lampa lamp
latać (to) fly
latarka flashlight
latarnia morska lighthouse
lawenda lavender
lew lion
linijka ruler
lis fox
liść leaf
liść klonu maple leaf
lodówka refrigerator
lody ice cream
lokomotywa engine
lornetka binoculars
ludzie people
lustro mirror

Ł

łata patch
ława bench
łokieć elbow
łopata shovel
łowić (to) fish
łódka boat
łóżko bed
łyżka spoon

M

magazyn magazine
magik magician
magnes magnet
malarz painter
malina raspberry
małpa monkey
mały small
mapa map

R

radio radio
rakieta racket; rocket
ramka frame
rekin shark
ręcznik towel
ręka hand
rękawiczka glove; mitten
robić na drutach (to) knit
rogi horns
rogi jelenie antlers
rower bicycle
rozgwiazda starfish
róża rose
ryba fish
rycerz knight
rynek marketplace
rysować (to) draw
ryś lynx
rzeka river
rzodkiewka radish

S

samochód car
samolot airplane
sałata lettuce
sanki sled
sarna deer
schody stairs
schody ruchome escalator
ser cheese
serce heart
siadać (to) sit
siano hay
siedem seven
sito sieve
skarpeta sock
sklepienie łukowe arch
składanka jigsaw puzzle
skoczyć (to) jump
skrzydła wings
skrzypce violin
słonecznik sunflower
słoń elephant
słońce sun
słowik nightingale

słowo word
słuchać (to) listen
smok dragon
sosna pine
sowa owl
sól salt
spać (to) sleep
spadochron parachute
stary old
statek ship
statek oceaniczny ocean liner
stopa foot
stół table
strach fear
struś ostrich
strzała arrow
sukienka dress
sweter sweater
szalik scarf
szczeniak puppy
szczotka brush
szeptać (to) whisper
sześć six
szklanka glass
szkoła school
sznur rope
szop raccoon
szpilka pin
szyć (to) sew
szyny tracks

Ś

ścieżka path
ślimak snail
śliwka plum
śmiech laughter
śniadanie breakfast

śnieg snow
śpiewać (to) sing
śrubokręt screwdriver
świeca candle
świnia pig

T

tablica ogłoszeń bulletin board
taca tray
taczka wheelbarrow
taksówka cab
talerz plate
tańczyć (to) dance
teatr theater
telewizja television
tęcza rainbow
torebka damska handbag
tort cake
toster toaster
tratwa raft
trąbka trumpet
truskawka strawberry
trzmiel bumblebee
trzy three
tukan toucan
tulipan tulip
tunel tunnel
twarz face
tygrys tiger

U

usta mouth
uścisnąć (to) hug
uśmiech smile

W

w górę uphill
wagon coach
waza vase
ważka dragonfly
ważyć (to) weigh
wąsy whiskers
wąż snake

welon veil
węzeł knot
wiadro bucket
wiatr wind
wiatrak fan
wiatrowskaz weather vane
wiązać (to) tie
widelec fork
wielbłąd camel
wieloryb whale
wieś village
wiewiórka squirrel
wieża tower
wilk wolf
winogrona grapes
wiosło oar
wiosłować (to) row
wiśnia cherry
wlewać (to) pour
wodospad waterfall
wół ox
wróbel sparrow
wspinać się (to) climb
wyspa island

Z

zamek castle; lock
zamiatać (to) sweep
zbierać (to) gather
zebra zebra
zegarek watch
zeszyt notebook
zielony green
ziemniak potato
zima winter
złota rybka goldfish
znaczek stamp

Ż

żaba frog
żeglować (to) sail
żakiet jacket
żarówka lightbulb
żelazko iron
żniwa harvest
żółty yellow
żółw turtle
żyrafa giraffe

Folk Tales from Bohemia
Adolf Wenig
This folk tale collection is one of a kind, focusing uniquely on humankind's struggle with evil in the world. Delicately ornate red and black text and illustrations set the mood.
Ages 9 and up
90 pages • red and black illustrations • 5 1/2 x 8 1/4 • 0-7818-0718-2 • W • $14.95hc • (786)

Czech, Moravian and Slovak Fairy Tales
Parker Fillmore
Fifteen different classic, regional folk tales and 23 charming illustrations whisk the reader to places of romance, deception, royalty, and magic.
Ages 12 and up
243 pages • 23 b/w illustrations • 5 1/2 x 8 1/4 • 0-7818-0714-X • W • $14.95 hc • (792)

Glass Mountain: Twenty-Eight Ancient Polish Folk Tales and Fables
W.S. Kuniczak
Illustrated by Pat Bargielski
As a child in a far-away misty corner of Volhynia, W.S. Kuniczak was carried away to an extraordinary world of magic and illusion by the folk tales of his Polish nurse.
171 pages • 6 x 9 • 8 illustrations • 0-7818-0552-X • W • $16.95hc • (645)

Old Polish Legends
Retold by F.C. Anstruther
Wood engravings by J. Sekalski
This fine collection of eleven fairy tales, with an introduction by Zymunt Nowakowski, was first published in Scotland during World War II.
66 pages • 7 1/4 x 9 • 11 woodcut engravings • 0-7818-0521-X • W • $11.95hc • (653)

Folk Tales from Russia
by Donald A. Mackenzie
With nearly 200 pages and 8 full-page black-and-white illustrations, the reader will be charmed by these legendary folk tales that symbolically weave magical fantasy with the historic events of Russia's past.
Ages 12 and up
192 pages • 8 b/w illustrations • 5 1/2 x 8 1/4 • 0-7818-0696-8 • W • $12.50hc • (788)

Fairy Gold: A Book of Classic English Fairy Tales
Chosen by Ernest Rhys
Illustrated by Herbert Cole
Forty-nine imaginative black and white illustrations accompany thirty classic tales, including such beloved stories as "Jack and the Bean Stalk" and "The Three Bears."
Ages 12 and up
236 pages • 5 1/2 x 8 1/4 • 49 b/w illustrations • 0-7818-0700-X • W • $14.95hc • (790)

Tales of Languedoc: From the South of France

Samuel Jacques Brun

For readers of all ages, here is a masterful collection of folk tales from the south of France.

Ages 12 and up

248 pages • 33 b/w sketches • 5 1/2 x 8 1/4 • 0-7818-0715-8 • W • $14.95hc • (793)

Twenty Scottish Tales and Legends

Edited by Cyril Swinson

Illustrated by Allan Stewart

Twenty enchanting stories take the reader to an extraordinary world of magic harps, angry giants, mysterious spells and gallant Knights.

Ages 9 and up

215 pages • 5 1/2 x 8 1/4 • 8 b/w illustrations • 0-7818-0701-8 • W • $14.95 hc • (789)

Swedish Fairy Tales

Translated by H. L. Braekstad

A unique blending of enchantment, adventure, comedy, and romance make this collection of Swedish fairy tales a must-have for any library.

Ages 9 and up

190 pages • 21 b/w illustrations • 51/2 x 81/4 • 0-7818-0717-4 • W • $12.50hc • (787)

The Little Mermaid and Other Tales

Hans Christian Andersen

Here is a near replica of the first American edition of 27 classic fairy tales from the masterful Hans Christian Andersen.

Ages 9 and up

508 pages • b/w illustrations • 6 x 9 • 0-7818-0720-4 • W • $19.95hc • (791)

Pakistani Folk Tales: Toontoony Pie and Other Stories

Ashraf Siddiqui and Marilyn Lerch

Illustrated by Jan Fairservis

In these 22 folk tales are found not only the familiar figures of folklore—kings and beautiful princesses—but the magic of the Far East, cunning jackals, and wise holy men.

Ages 7 and up

158 pages • 6 1/2 x 8 1/2 • 38 illustrations • 0-7818-0703-4 • W • $12.50hc • (784)

Folk Tales from Chile

Brenda Hughes

This selection of 15 tales gives a taste of the variety of Chile's rich folklore. Fifteen charming illustrations accompany the text.

Ages 7 and up

121 pages • 5 1/2 x 8 1/4 • 15 illustrations • 0-7818-0712-3 • W • $12.50hc • (785)

All prices subject to change. **To purchase Hippocrene Books** contact your local bookstore, call (718) 454-2366, or write to: HIPPOCRENE BOOKS, 171 Madison Avenue, New York, NY 10016. Please enclose check or money order, adding $5.00 shipping (UPS) for the first book and $.50 for each additional book.